MW01144403

Trails of
Fredericton

Bill Thorpe

GOOSE LANE EDITIONS
FREDERICTON TRAILS COALITION

© William W. Thorpe, 1999.
Maps courtesy of the City of Fredericton and Kingswood.

Edited by Darrell Mesheau and Laurel Boone.
Cover photographs by Harold Boone (top, bottom and background)
and Keith Minchin (centre).
Cover and book design by Ryan Astle.
Printed in Canada by Transcontinental Printing.
10 9 8 7 6 5 4 3 2 1

Published with the financial support of the Government of
Canada, through the Book Publishing Industry Development
Program, and the New Brunswick Department of Economic
Development, Tourism and Culture.

Canadä

Canadian Cataloguing in Publication Data

Thorpe, Bill, 1933-
   Trails of Fredericton

   Includes bibliographical references and index.
   ISBN 0-86492-235-3

1. Trails — New Brunswick — Fredericton — Guidebooks.
2. Hiking — New Brunswick — Fredericton — Guidebooks.
3. Fredericton (N.B.) — Guidebooks. I. Title.

GV199.44.C22F74 1999   796.51′09715′515
C99-950118-6

Goose Lane Editions   Fredericton Trails Coalition
469 King Street   PO Box 3715, Station B
Fredericton, New Brunswick   Fredericton, New Brunswick
CANADA E3B 1E5   CANADA E3A 5L7

This book is dedicated to all trail users and trail builders. It acknowledges our historical debt to the Maliseet people; to the early European settlers who walked the trails and paddled the streams; to the railwaymen who left a legacy of labour and a network to build on; and to my colleagues in the Fredericton Trails Coalition, particularly Harold Boone, John Gilbert, Paul Gorman, George Hubbard, Carolyn Jones, Vern Smith, and Patty Trail, who have pursued the common goal with dedication and humour.

The scarlet of the maples can shake me like a cry
Of bugles going by.
And my lonely spirit thrills
To see the frosty asters like a smoke upon the hills.

— *from* "A Vagabond Song," Bliss Carman

When they were young, Bliss Carman and his cousin, Charles G.D. Roberts, often tramped the woods around Fredericton, sometimes accompanied by their teacher, George R. Parkin, the Headmaster of the Collegiate School from 1871 until 1889. Fredericton became "The Poets' Corner of Canada" partly due to these rambles. Our trail system is an attempt to preserve, near the end of the 20th century, some features of the Fredericton they knew and loved. The beauty of our trails, particularly in the fall, can indeed still shake us "like a cry of bugles going by."

Table of Contents

Foreword

Once, when I was twelve years old, I awoke to see clouds lying in the valleys of the White Mountains. I had walked up Mount Hayes to camp on the blueberry-fringed ledges near the summit. Now the fiery morning sun painted peaks in golden rays, their grey stone crowns thrust up through the cottony fields of heaven like islands adrift in primordial mists. The clouds, I thought, have lain in the valleys so as not to drift away on night-time winds.

By now you are wondering how my experiences in the White Mountains of New Hampshire relate to Fredericton's trails. The connection is basic; the common element is the adventure of walking. That said, one does not need to awake to the sight of morning clouds settled in green valleys to appreciate a good walk. An early morning trip across an old railroad bridge over the mist-shrouded St. John River can be as spiritually and physically fulfilling as any walk to any place.

Walking rejuvenates the soul. Where you walk does not seem to be nearly as important as the fact that you simply do it. I'm not talking about the functional process that takes me to the photocopier or bathroom. I speak of moving over the landscape as an experience of both physical and spiritual significance.

I imagine my ancestors.

The Maliseet walked the forested valleys of the Wulustuk long before settlers from afar chose this place as their new home. Their appreciation of the ability to walk was from a different perspective. In order to take advantage of seasonal economic opportunities, the

Maliseet had to be mobile. Walking must have been a form of ancient ritual dedicated to survival.

As you walk the trails of Fredericton and consider the history that surrounds them, don't forget to look beyond the buildings, bridges and roadways to the distant past. The woodlands and river shores of the "Celestial City" have changed over time. Now, my own ancestral connections, although much older, resemble the sentiments of many contemporary Frederictonians.

Here is life.
Sustenance and shelter.
Home.

I do not believe that one can ever experience all the sights and sounds of any single path in a lifetime. There are four major changes to the landscape in one year, many more in a decade. To look around carefully is to see new things and find what was not there the last time you came this way.

Bill Thorpe knows these things, too. His ancestors also walked, with equal consideration for the spiritual and physical benefits. Walk with him now as he tells what he has seen and heard from the trails of the "Celestial City."

You may find beautiful clouds of imagination lying in the valleys of your mind.

Patrick Polchies
Fredericton, 1999

Introduction

The Fredericton Trails Coalition

Fredericton Trails Coalition, Inc. (FTC), is a non-profit, voluntary public service organization dedicated to the preservation, development, and promotion of green spaces. Its objectives are:

1. To assist in the coordination of a system of trails in the Greater Fredericton Area which would provide trail recreation opportunities for a wide range of users.
2. To inform the general public about the advantages which such a trail system has to offer.
3. To form an advisory coalition of all organizations and agencies that support these goals.

Two major issues attracted the attention of Frederictonians to the need for a formally organized association to maintain the trails that already existed within the city and to turn other property into trails accessible to the public. First, in the late 1970s, the city decided to build the Westmorland Street Bridge to replace the old Carleton Street Bridge, which could no longer accommodate the city's cross-river traffic. Then City Council had to figure out what to do with the Carleton Street Bridge. Some councillors wished to retain it as a pedestrian and cycle bridge. They and their supporters argued that a trust fund could be set up, and that this, together with a yearly rental fee which the New Brunswick Electric Power Commission was prepared to pay to run its lines across the river, would create sufficient income to maintain the bridge. However, this plan was not to be. Council voted instead to remove the superstructure of the Carleton Street Bridge at a cost of $750,000; the piers were left in place because removal would have cost an additional $1,000,000. Perhaps at that time it was a "bridge too far," or, to put it another way, perhaps Fredericton had to lose a bridge to gain a bridge at a later date.

A second bone of contention that prompted the establishment of the Fredericton Trails Coalition was what has become the Valley Trail. The Valley Line of the Saint John & Quebec Railway had been abandoned in 1967, and by the 1980s, the use of the right of way was in dispute. Patty Trail began a mission to explore the possibility of a scenic, safe, and natural trail from the Woodstock Road to Mactaquac. She found that the abandoned rail line from the Golf Club Road to McIntosh Brook, which marks the city limits, had been purchased by the City of Fredericton, and that the New Brunswick Electric Power Commission owned the remainder of the right of way from McIntosh Brook to Mactaquac. Patty persuaded the Kiwanis Club of Fredericton, under its president, Walter J. Dohaney, to invest a large sum of money in making the Valley Trail a viable proposition. She was ably supported in this endeavour by city staff members Richard Danziger and Jim McElman and Councillor Gerry Ward. However, some of the residents whose property adjoined the right of way disputed its use as a trail, and the fat was in the fire. To avoid controversy, the Kiwanis Club withdrew its offer. The city itself was not prepared to pursue the matter in the courts, which is what it would have had to do to represent the broad interests of the City of Fredericton against the interests of a few individuals.

At this point, Fredericton Heritage Trust and its president, Penny Ericson, entered the picture. Penny took the point of view that the mission statement of Fredericton Heritage Trust — that it be concerned with the "built and natural heritage" of the city — clearly expressed a mandate to preserve this trail for the citizens. She fought and won the case; however, the judge, in rendering his decision, asked the city to offer the residents along the abandoned railway right of way the opportunity to secure 10-year leases. A number chose to do so; the last of these leases will expire in 2002. When it does, the Valley Trail will be complete to the city limits at McIntosh Brook. Negotiations are continuing to extend the Valley Trail beyond the city limits to Mactaquac.

An early relationship was thus established between Fredericton Heritage Trust and those who wished to take care of Fredericton's trails. Some members of Fredericton Heritage Trust felt that an organization specifically devoted to trails was needed, and thus the Fredericton Trails Coalition came into being. An interim board of directors was elected in May, 1990, and the Coalition has continued to grow since that date. By 1998, the active member groups included the Fredericton Freewheelers, the Capital City Road Runners, the Outdoor Enthusiasts of Fredericton, and the Wostawea Ski Club.

David Peterson and I were among the charter members of this new organization, which became a standard-bearer for trails among municipalities in this province. In turn, David founded and became the first president of the New Brunswick Trails Council, in which the Fredericton Trails Coalition has been an active participant. Patty Trail, the eloquent spokesperson for the Valley Trail, became one of the first members of the Fredericton Trails Coalition, and Marion Cumming, a devoted member of Fredericton Heritage Trust and a well-known Fredericton artist, designed the logo.

In 1979, the City of Fredericton had designated the trails outside the previously established park system as "linear park" and had given them the protection of special bylaws. By 1998, the linear park system consisted of over 50 kilometres of trails.

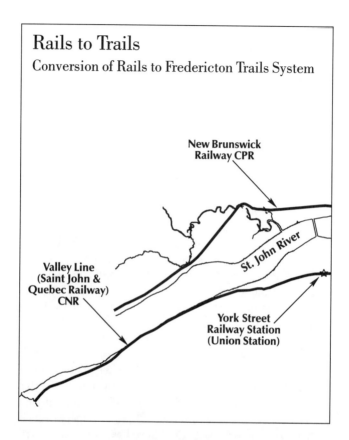

Rails to Trails
Conversion of Rails to Fredericton Trails System

New Brunswick
Railway CPR

St. John River

Valley Line
(Saint John &
Quebec Railway)
CNR

York Street
Railway Station
(Union Station)

Using *Trails of Fredericton*

The majority of Fredericton's trails utilize former railbeds. Thus the grades are not severe, and the pathway has been made smooth with a crusher dust surface. Generally a 3.05-metre (10-foot) width is maintained both summer and winter. Most trails are suitable for wheelchair use.

I have estimated the difficulty of these trails — from easy to strenuous — according to the guidelines set out by Marianne Eiselt and H.A. Eiselt in *A Hiking Guide to New Brunswick*, 2nd Edition (Goose Lane, 1996). Most

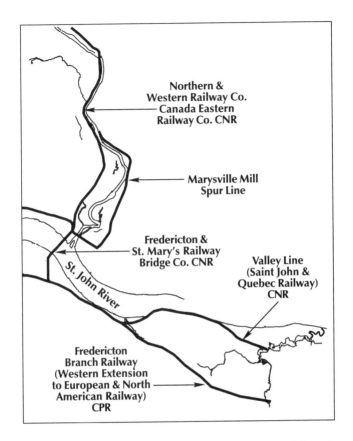

of the Fredericton linear park system is easy, with length being the chief factor in measuring the level of difficulty. The trails in the upper reaches of Odell Park, which is not in the linear park system, are an example of more difficult terrain: the paths are narrow, ungroomed, un-surfaced, and, because of changes in elevation, somewhat steep.

The distances indicated at the beginning of each trail description measure the trail from beginning to end, one way. The hiking times are based on a comfortable pace for the walker of average ability. Fredericton Trails Coalition members did actual, on-foot, on-trail research over a period of several days in all weather conditions (except snow) to determine that 12 minutes per kilometre is a reasonable average walking speed on these trails.

In 1998, a Trail Patrol was created to provide "eyes and ears" for the trail system. The New Brunswick Trails Council has given guidance in setting up this voluntary organization, which operates under the umbrella of the City of Fredericton and the city police force's community police program. Up to a hundred volunteers will be required, and regulations governing such matters as uniforms and duties are being formulated.

Useful Tips for Trails Users
All users:
1.   Obey all signs.
2.   Leave nothing but footprints.
3.   Stay on the designated trails.

Cyclists
1.   Give way to walkers and joggers.
2.   Travel single file.
3.   Obey posted speed limits: usually 15 km/h on trails and 10 km/h on bridges.
4.   Bicycles must be equipped with bells.
5.   Cyclists must wear helmets.
6.   Avoid drain grates, soft shoulders, and other surface hazards on trails and where trails cross streets.

Motorized vehicles

1. Motorized vehicles are not permitted on the trails.
2. In 1998, on a trial basis, City Council permitted limited access to a short section of the Marysville/Nashwaak Trail so that snowmobilers might gain access to a bridge crossing the Nashwaak River. This policy was reaffirmed for the 1998-1999 winter season and may or may not be reinstated as circumstances warrant. Please check with Harold Boone, Foreman, Parks and Trees Division, Fredericton City Hall (460-2230) before driving a snowmobile over this stretch of trail.

Dogs

1. Dogs must be kept on leash at all times.
2. The "Stoop and Scoop" bylaw must be observed summer and winter. Waste recep-

RAILWAY	FINISHED
F'ton Branch Rwy (Western Extension to European & North American Rwy: Saint John-Vanceboro ME)	1869
York St. Rwy Stn (F'ton Branch) York St. Rwy Stn Union Station	1869 1923 1938
Saint John & Quebec Rwy (Valley Line: Saint John-Centreville)	1919
F'ton & St. Mary's Rwy Bridge Co. Rebuilt	1888 1938
Central Rwy, NB Coal Rwy, F'ton & Grand Lake Rwy	1913
Marysville Mill Spur	1913
Northern & Western Rwy Co. (Canada Eastern Rwy Co., 1890), S. Devon-Chatham	1887
NB Rwy Co., Gibson (Devon)-Edmundston	1878

CONVERSION

LATER NAME(S)	ABANDONED	TRAIL
NB Rwy Co. (1993) CPR (1890)	1993	Pending
CPR	1924	Pending
	1962 (pass.) (CNR) 1985 (pass.) 1990 (freight)	Pending
CNR (1929)	1967 (Above F'ton) 1984 (Oromocto-Westfield) 1995 (total)	Lincoln (8.8 km) 1997 Valley (9.4 km) 1993
Cdn Gov't Rwy (1905) CNR (1924)	1995	St. John River Pedestrian Bridge (581m) 1997
CPR (1913)	1986	Pending
CPR (1914)	1982*	Gibson (4.1 km) 1993
Cdn Gov't Rwy (1905) CNR (1924)	1985 (McGivney-Newcastle) 1995 (McGivney-Fredericton)	Marysville/Nashwaak (7.44 km) 1997
CPR (1890)	1992	North Side (10.2 km) 1996

*Canadian Pacific Railway Archives records show 1982 as the date of abandonment, but the Canadian Transportation Agency gives the year of abandonment as 1986, the year in which the Minto Subdivision (above) was also abandoned.

Alexander "Boss" Gibson and Frederick B. Edgecombe view the first railway flanger ever used, invented by John Hamilton, a black blacksmith. The photograph looks west at the corner of present-day York and Aberdeen streets, with the second Exhibition Palace (1869-1877) in the background. The railway line is not part of any trail yet but may provide the link between the Valley Trail and the Lincoln Trail. PANB P5-373, GEORGE T. TAYLOR COLLECTION

A passenger train at the Marysville Station, December 26, 1955. WALTER LONG

A Canadian Pacific train crossing the Barker's Point Bridge, now a pedestrian walkway, in 1987. BRIAN BARCHARD

A Canadian Pacific train passing the Friel Street crossing in North Devon and approaching the Westmorland Street Bridge underpass (1981). BRIAN BARCHARD

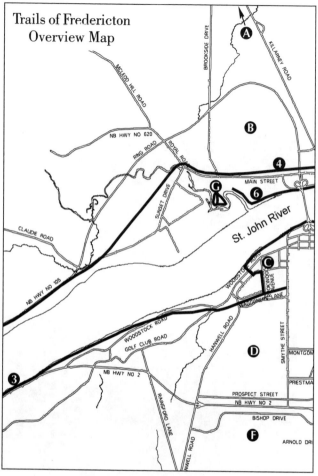

FREDERICTON AREA TRAILS

1. Salamanca (0.7 km)
2. The Green (4.0 km)
3. Valley Trail (9.4 km)
4. North Side (10.2 km)
5. Gibson (4.1 km)
6. Riverfront Pathway (2.0 km)
7. Marysville/Nashwaak (7.4 km)
8. The Hub (0.9 km)
9. Lincoln (8.8 km)

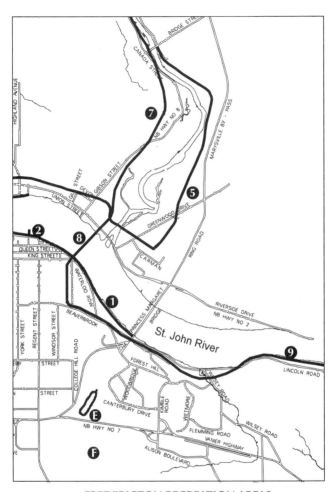

FREDERICTON RECREATION AREAS

A. Killarney Lake
B. Nashwaaksis Field House
C. Wilmot Park
D. Odell Park
E. Reading Street Park
F. UNB Woodlot & Game Refuge
G. Johnston Avenue Environmental Park

Historic view of the Fredericton Railway Bridge from Fredericton North. The railway car in the foreground bears the name Northern & Western Railway, the original name of the Canada Eastern Branch of the Canadian National Railway system, which went from Fredericton to Newcastle and Chatham. The upriver pier near the opposite bank assisted in operating the swing span. The wharf on the near shore was reputed to have been partially built with planks from old Fort Nashwaak. PANB P5-427

South Side

The Buttery, Old Government House. HAROLD BOONE

The Hub Pedestrian Bridge. CITY OF FREDERICTON, TOURISM

The Valley Trail. HAROLD BOONE

The Hub

Length: 581 m   **Wheelchair Use:** yes
Difficulty: easy   **Direction:** north - south
Hiking Time: 10 min

The Hub is the junction of a number of trails. At a beautiful location on the Green, on the banks of the St. John River and within sight of Christ Church Cathedral, its distinguishing features include the Fredericton Railway Bridge and the Trans Canada Trail Pavilion.

Fredericton was the third community to have a Trans Canada Trail Pavilion, a red-roofed design now recognizable across Canada; each pavilion indicates a significant point on the Trans Canada Trail. This 15,000-kilometre trail is the longest in the world, extending from the Atlantic Ocean to the Pacific Ocean and following the Mackenzie River northward to the Arctic Ocean.

The lists emblazoned on the plaques on the Pavilion wall contain the names of individuals, firms, and organizations who have helped finance the trail, a recognition that ensures citizen participation and stewardship. Individuals may claim a metre of trail for $40 and have their names or a dedication inscribed on the plaque (see Useful Addresses, page 97). The Trail Pavilion was opened in 1997, and a second plaque, containing hundreds more names, was unveiled in 1998.

A significant trail contributor was J.D. Irving Ltd., which donated 377 kilometres of railbed from Grand Falls downriver to Fredericton. Known as the Irving Trail, it forms a significant part of the Trans Canada Trail's New Brunswick section. (At the Fredericton city limits, it is also called the North Side Trail.) It crosses the Fredericton Railway Bridge at the Hub and proceeds downriver via the Lincoln Trail.

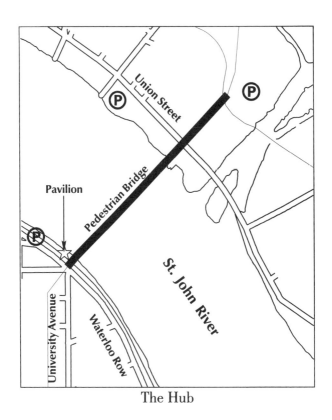

The Hub

The Bridge

Frederictonians and visitors beat a path across the river via the Hub on almost a daily basis. Up to 300 people may be found on the bridge at any one point in time during good weather, particularly in the evenings, and even winter use is heavy because the trail is groomed. Next to the Boyce Farmers' Market on Saturday mornings, the Fredericton Railway Bridge is no doubt the most popular "people place" in Fredericton. I walk or cycle the bridge, rain or shine, at least twice a week.

The history of the bridge is very much a history of

The Hub's distinguishing features include the Fredericton Railway Bridge and the Trans Canada Trail Pavilion. BILL THORPE

the railway and the railwaymen of what has become a bygone era. The original railway bridge was constructed by the Fredericton and St. Marys Railway Bridge Company in 1888 to accommodate the expanding railway network which had reached Fredericton about 20 years earlier. By 1924, it had become part of the Canadian National system and was used by the Canadian Pacific Railway as well. The first bridge was carried away by the spring freshet and ice jam of 1936, but the second was in operation again at a higher elevation by 1938. The single pier upriver was placed there in conjunction with the swing span that enabled the passage of high-masted ships. The swing span last operated to allow a dredge upriver to assist in building the Westmorland Street Bridge in the early 1980s. It is no longer operational.

A description of the bridge must be accompanied by a mention of at least a few of the tragedies which occurred here. One involved a railwayman by the name of Joe Lewis. He was assisting in the operation of the draw span to let the riverboat, *D.J. Purdy*, through. After the boat had passed and the span was locked in place, he slipped and fell to his death.

No doubt the most heroic event that took place on the bridge occurred on Remembrance Day, November 11, 1945. Professor Bryan Priestman of the University of New Brunswick was on the bridge that day when 8-year-old Ronald Dempsey fell off. Professor Priestman must have known that the cold water of the St. John River offered little hope for survival at that time of year, yet he plunged in after the child. Both lives were lost. UNB commemorates his heroism by an annual lecture given in his name. The bridge stands as a silent tribute.

In April, 1995, the last train crossed the bridge, and by 1997 it was planked by Sentier NB Trail with the assistance of the City of Fredericton, finally permitting people to walk across the bridge and legitimizing what many practical Northsiders had been doing illegally, and dangerously, for years to reach downtown. Most of the financing came from the provincial and federal governments. The bridge is 581 metres (1906 feet) in length, making it the longest pedestrian bridge in the world converted from a railway bridge. The Fredericton Trails Coalition brochure gives the length as 900 metres, a measurement that includes the bridge itself and approach sections. The opening ceremony of the bridge and the Trans Canada Trail Pavilion on New Brunswick Day, August 4, 1997, was attended by thousands.

Splendid views up and down the river and of the north and south sides of the city are obtained from all points on the bridge. There are two viewing platforms facing upriver and one facing downriver, providing wonderful photo opportunities. A number of Y's Men associations provided the funding for the downriver platform.

During the summer of 1998 several public-spirited

firms and organizations contributed funds for the lighting of the bridge. The lights were turned on for the first time on June 6, Trans Canada Trail Day. Each firm is honoured with a separate plaque, and the Fredericton Trails Coalition marked the occasion with a plaque of its own mounted near the downriver platform. A ramp is to be built at the north end of the bridge in the summer of 1999 to connect with Carleton Park.

Parking

Parking is available for the Hub on Queen, King, Church, and other side streets, some of it metered. Pay careful attention to posted signs for parking restrictions. On the North Side, parking is available at Carleton Park or near Barker Street.

The Salamanca Trail

Length: 1.0 km + 0.7 km **Wheelchair Use:** yes,
Difficulty: easy   except for end grades
Hiking Time: 20 min   **Direction:** west - east
     + 15 min

To reach the Salamanca Trail, which is about 700 metres long, you start at the Hub by the Railway Bridge and the Trail Pavilion, walk through the underpass, and continue eastward downriver for about a kilometre along a lovely stretch of the Green. This section of the Green parallels Waterloo Row, running between that street and the river and offering views of some of the most beautiful older homes in eastern Canada.

Waterloo Row is, of course, named for the victory of the Duke of Wellington over Napoleon at Waterloo in present-day Belgium in 1815. The entire housing area on

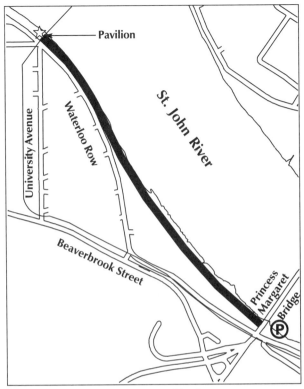

Salamanca Trail

view from this part of the trail is part of a newly created preservation district, the St. Anne's Point Heritage Preservation Area. In this neighbourhood are some of New Brunswick's finest old houses, most of them dating from the 19th century and a very few from the 18th.

The building at 12-14 Waterloo Row, immediately after the underpass, was originally McLeod's Inn. Built in 1788, it is the only survivor of the 18th-century inns along Fredericton's waterfront; it is one of the city's oldest houses. Riverboats bearing romantic names like

Waterloo Row during the Great Flood of 1887. The steamer and woodboat are tied up near McLeod's Inn. PANB P5-349A GEORGE T. TAYLOR COLLECTION

Reindeer, Forest Queen, Water Witch, and *May Queen* began plying the St. John River in 1816 and continued to do so until 1946. Many stopped along Waterloo Row, and the landing in front of this establishment was called McLeod's Corner. This house, like the other houses in the area, recently received a measure of protection with the 1997 preservation bylaw.

The house at 38 Waterloo Row was a 19th-century inn and tavern, the Royal Oak, and Fredericton's first inn, the Golden Ball Inn, was located just upriver from 58 Waterloo Row. While it no longer exists, from 1867 until 1869 the Golden Ball was the home of the distinguished Victorian writer, Juliana Horatia Ewing, whose works refer to it as "Reka Dom" (Russian for *river house*), and whose writing produced the symbolism used by the Brownies. Her husband, Major Alexander Ewing, who wrote the hymn "Jerusalem the Golden," was organist at the Cathedral while they lived here.

Number 58, a large white Classical Revival house distinguished by its Ionic capital pillars and built about 1910, has been the residence of a judge, a federal cabinet minister, a premier, and two lieutenant-governors, and it is now the residence of the president of the University of New Brunswick. The university flag often flies over the porch.

On the downriver corner of Shore Street and Waterloo Row is a house built around 1790 and marked by a plaque which reads:

> Land originally granted to Benedict Arnold. The home, 1812-1858, of Colonel George Shore, Surveyor-General of New Brunswick. Home of Senator Muriel McQueen-Fergusson, first woman Speaker of the Senate of Canada.

Senator McQueen-Fergusson, founder of the Muriel McQueen-Fergusson Foundation, which engendered the Muriel McQueen-Fergusson Centre for Family Violence Research, died in 1997. It is interesting to note that Benedict Arnold, someone who might be described as the senator's antithesis in terms of amiability and honesty, did indeed live in Fredericton, though not at this property, and was apparently forced to leave in 1787 after his unappealing ways disgraced him among the citizenry here.

Carrying on downriver, the large white house at 238 Waterloo Row is known as Somerville House. With its expansive grounds and three flagpoles, it was the residence of the lieutenant-governors of New Brunswick from 1975 until 1999. This house was once owned by Lord Beaverbrook, a native New Brunswicker and noted British newspaper publisher. As Minister of Aircraft Production in Winston Churchill's World War II government, he was instrumental in securing victory in the aerial Battle of Britain. The lieutenant-governor moved to the newly refurbished Old Government House on Woodstock Road in 1999.

To the left are the Morell Park baseball field and two

The covered bridge on the Salamanca Trail. RYAN ASTLE

soccer pitches. Hard as it is to imagine in the summer, the goal posts are often covered by the spring freshet to within centimetres of their crossbars.

The Salamanca Trail

The beginning of the Salamanca Trail is not exactly defined, but opposite where Alexandra Street meets Waterloo Row there is a large stone cairn which reads:

> That Ye May Tell It to the Generations Following
> . . . . Unveiling took place Oct. 8, 1933, the one
> hundred and fiftieth anniversary of the arrival in
> this location of a company of United Empire
> Loyalists, some of whom are buried in the nearby
> cemetery, having died from the effects of cold
> and privation suffered during the first winter
> here.

Ask any number of Frederictonians where the Green ends and the Salamanca Trail begins, and you will get any number of answers. My answer is, the trail begins at the cairn.

Soon after the cairn, the trail descends down a roadway past the Morell Park ball diamond, with a boat launching beach dead ahead and a parking lot on the right. The trail, for a time, follows the roadway to the right into the trees along the river.

Salamanca is the area of Fredericton at the downriver end of Waterloo Row. It traces its name to a battle fought in 1812 during the Peninsular War near Salamanca, Spain, between the British under the Duke of Wellington and the French forces of Napoleon. This path leads even further back into history than that.

On the right, after the trees begin and just before the brick transfer station, is a short, secluded path which leads slightly uphill to the Loyalist Provincials' Burial Ground. The Loyalists were Americans who remained loyal to the king and fled the United States following the American Revolution; the Americans called them Tories. A commemorative monument attests to the hardships they suffered upon arrival, particularly during the first winter, 1783-1784, when most stayed in tents near the landing place. The Loyalist men, women, and children who did not survive that first winter are buried here. Most markers were of wood and have long since disappeared, but one rude stone remains in the Burial Ground.

Hannah Ingraham, when a girl of 11, came with her Loyalist family to Fredericton (then called Ste Anne) in October of 1783 and landed near the present location of the trail. In her diary she wrote:

> We lived in a tent at St. Ann's till father got a log house raised. He went up through our lot till he found a nice fresh spring of water, ... so there he built his house. One morning when we

waked up we found the snow deep on the ground all round us, and then father came wading through it and told us the house was ready and not to stop and light a fire then, and not mind the weather, but follow his tracks through the trees, for the trees were so many we soon lost sight of him going up the hill; it was snowing fast, and oh, so cold. Father carried a chest and we all took something and followed him up the hill through the trees. It was not long before we heard him pounding, and oh, what a joy to see our gable end. There was no floor laid, no window, no chimney, no door, but we had a roof at last. A good fire was blazing on the hearth, and mother had a big loaf of bread with us, and she boiled a kettle of water and put a good piece of butter in a pewter bowl . . . and mother said, "Thank God, we are no longer in dread of having shots fired through our house. This is the sweetest meal I have tasted for many a day."

This description is not, of course, something that can be seen from the trail, but this was the locale of which she wrote, and this is a trail through history. At a later date the British Garrison sometimes held mock skirmishes on the Green and in the Salamanca area.

The trail is at flood-plain level and is usually covered during spring freshet and even during long periods of heavy rainfall. Shortly after passing the transfer station on the high ground to the right, it crosses a stream called Earle Creek, named after Fredericton's first doctor, Dr. Charles Earle, who arrived as a Loyalist with the New Jersey Volunteers. As children living near its upper reaches some kilometres away on York Street, we merely called it "The Brook." City maps sometimes refer to it rather prosaically as the Back Drain. During my youth it flowed almost its entire length above-ground, and, in winter, we skated to the river, often stopping in the Frogmore area, near the foot of the hill on Regent Street, to play hockey. We collected tadpoles in the brook in the early summer before it dried up. Today the brook mainly flows through underground pipes.

Farther along the trail, a covered bridge has been constructed by city work crews. At its lower end the Salamanca Trail emerges into an open area closer to the river, passing several newer homes and then continuing uphill under the Princess Margaret Bridge. Here you can connect with the Lincoln Trail by crossing the Lincoln Road near Dunns Crossing Road. Dunns Crossing is a former railway crossing, now a trail crossing, named after a long-time resident, a coal and wood merchant by the name of Dickie Dunn, who lived nearby on a dead-end road; his firm went by the name of R.U. Dunn.

Parking

Parking is available in four areas: by the Green along Queen Street at meters just upriver from the Trail Pavilion; on the side streets off Waterloo Row; near the boat launching beach in Morell Park; and at the downriver end of the trail in the open area under the Princess Margaret Bridge.

The Lincoln Trail

Length: 8.8 km   **Wheelchair Use:** yes
Difficulty: easy   **Direction:** west - east
Hiking Time: 2 hr

The Lincoln Trail begins at the Hub at the south end of the Railway Bridge and is a continuation of the trail from

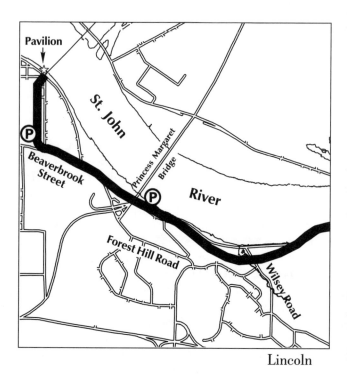

Lincoln

the bridge as it moves southward after crossing the St. John River.

Straight off the bridge, with Christ Church Cathedral on the right, you will cross Brunswick, George, and Charlotte streets. All these streets, first named in 1819, bear royal associations and are in the original Town Platt of Fredericton. This area, designated in 1785, consisted of the land bounded by Queen Street, University Avenue (then Sunbury Street), Charlotte Street, and Smythe Street. Most of Fredericton's older homes are to be found in this area, and a large portion of the eastern section is part of the St. Anne's Point Heritage Preservation Area.

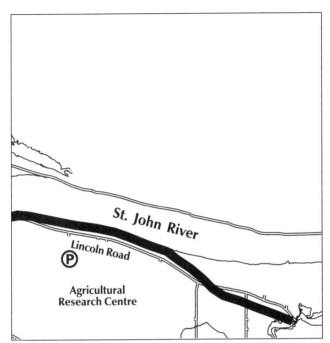

Trail

As you proceed along the Lincoln Trail beyond George and Charlotte streets, which were brought down to grade level in 1998, you will see the clock tower of the Lady Beaverbrook Residence almost in line with the trail straight ahead. The musical system in the bell tower, seldom heard today, used to play one of Lord Beaverbrook's favourite Miramichi songs, "The Jones Boys."

Beyond Charlotte Street, the fenced playing field on the right is College Field, a bequest from the estate of Edward H. Wilmot in 1896. On the other side of the trail is the Lord Beaverbrook Rink, a gift from "The Beaver" to the city in the 1950s.

The Canada Eastern Station in 1903. This station stood at the beginning of the Lincoln Trail at the south end of the Fredericton Railway Bridge, near Brunswick Street. From 1890 until 1933, the "Suburban" ran from this station to Sandyville, near Marysville, three times daily. The station was demolished in the 1960s and has been replaced by an apartment building. PANB P37-503, GEORGE T. TAYLOR COLLECTION

The trail now turns in a more easterly direction as it approaches University Avenue and the gates of the University of New Brunswick. The Fredericton Trails Coalition is presently working to extend this trail westward across town to cross Regent, York, Westmorland, and Northumberland streets and connect with the Valley Trail at Smythe Street. Hopefully, the abandoned York Street Railway Station, formerly Union Station, will be retained and form part of the extension.

If you leave the trail and turn up University Avenue, you will pass through the gates of the university. The University of New Brunswick was founded in 1785 by United Empire Loyalists and is the oldest provincial university in Canada. Today it has an enrolment of 6800 full-time students. From the trail, you can catch a glimpse of the grey stone Old Arts Building on the UNB campus beyond the gates. It is presently used for administrative purposes and houses a permanent display showing aspects of the school's history, although I attended classes there as late as the 1950s. Built in 1828, it is the oldest university building still in use in Canada.

In the 1960s, St. Thomas University moved from Chatham to Fredericton, and now, with 1800 full-time students, it sits on the summit of College Hill, above the UNB campus. St. Thomas, home of the Atlantic Human Rights Centre, the Third Age Centre, and the experimental Black Box Theatre, is not visible from the trail, nor is much of the UNB campus. The hill into the campuses is steep, but it is well worth the climb to see them and the views of the city and the river they afford. Several of the 50-odd buildings on campus can be visited, including the Old Arts Building, the William Brydone Jack Observatory, the Provincial Archives of New Brunswick, and the UNB Art Centre.

After the Lincoln Trail crosses University Avenue, it proceeds eastward, parallel with Beaverbrook Street, crossing a major intersection in the Salamanca area, where Beaverbrook Street, Waterloo Row, and Forest Hill Road all meet. It is not difficult to imagine the congestion that might have existed when the trail, in its previous incarnation as a railway, added trains to this busy traffic confluence.

Further along, at Dunns Crossing Road, the trail passes under the Princess Margaret Bridge, part of the Trans-Canada Highway, and the Salamanca Trail joins it from the left.

Shortly after Dunns Crossing Road, the trail becomes double. The upper half, closer to the hill, was the former Fredericton Branch Railway from Fredericton to Fredericton Junction, a branch of the Western Extension of the European and North American Railway, later part of the CPR network. It awaits improvement for trail purposes.

The Lincoln Trail runs close to the river at an elevation which provides excellent views. BILL THORPE

The lower half was the Valley Line of the Saint John and Quebec Railway and, later, part of the CNR system. It has now become the Lincoln Trail.

Just before the trail crosses the Lincoln Road at the foot of the Agriculture Canada Research Centre hill and swings closer to the river, you may wish to take advantage of the extensive public picnic facilities just up the slope on the grounds of the Experimental Farm. Besides parking space, there are two large picnic sites, barbecue pits and washroom facilities; these are open from 8:15 a.m. to 4:30 p.m. seven days a week during the summer months. The farm itself is well worth a visit, with its carefully manicured grounds and floral displays.

Beyond this crossing there is limited parking and limited access until the next crossing of the Lincoln Road, three kilometres further along. A covered picnic table was constructed in 1997 near the first Lincoln Road crossing as a Youth Services Canada project, with Fredericton Trails Coalition as one of the working partners.

From here the trail runs close to the river at an elevation which provides magnificent viewing. It carries on to the city limits at Lincoln. In the summer of 1998, it was useable but not crusher-dusted beyond the second crossing of the Lincoln Road. Regular users of this trail warn that there is heavy insect infestation during the spring and early summer. Otherwise this is a most enjoyable trail and comes highly recommended by its users.

Parking

There is ample parking near the Lady Beaverbrook Rink and in an adjacent parking lot enclosed by a hedge facing University Avenue. A large parking area exists near the confluence of the Salamanca and the Lincoln trails under the Princess Margaret Bridge. You'll find parking at the Experimental Farm picnic area and limited parking where the trail crosses the road in Lincoln near Aquarius Drive.

The Green

Length: 4.0 km
Difficulty: easy
Hiking Time: 45 min

Wheelchair Use: yes
Direction: east - west

The Green is the most popular and the most historical of the Fredericton trails. It is readily accessed from downtown Fredericton and presents an easy opportunity for a very pleasant 10-minute stroll during lunch hour or a full 45-minute walk at any time. Only the Railway Bridge carries more traffic on a regular basis. I suggest that your walk begin at the south end of the Railway Bridge by the Trans Canada Trail Pavilion and then proceed upriver. The portion of the Green below the Railway Bridge is described with the Salamanca Trail; see pages 32-39.

The Green presents a grand vista of the St. John

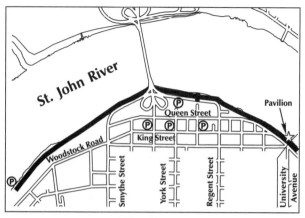

The Green

River. Just upstream from the Railway Bridge, the Nashwaak River enters the St. John River. These river systems
formed, in essence, the first trails. They had been used
by the Maliseet long before the settlement of the area
by the French. This use carried over into the French
period and beyond. The birch bark canoe was the main
vehicle of transportation and communication.

In 1692 the French king's emissary, Villebon, built Fort
St. Joseph, or Fort Nashwaak, at the mouth of the
Nashwaak near the site of the present-day Irving Oil tanks,
visible across the river from the Green. From the fort the
French and their Indian allies launched raids on British
settlements in New England. Villebon declared the area
the capital of Acadia, and the fort offered protection to
the village of Ste Anne, which grew up on the plains on
the South Side and continued to grow even after the fort
was abandoned in 1698. Part of the Green once formed
the river front of the village. In the winter of 1759, the
village was destroyed and its 147 buildings burned by a
New England raiding force led by Moses Hazen.

The Loyalists arrived in 1783. Fredericton was well

The Green. CORRIE ASTLE

situated, being some distance upriver from Saint John, which was more open to attack by sea, and also much nearer the centre of the province. These were the decisive factors in Governor Thomas Carleton's choice of Fredericton as the capital when New Brunswick was separated from Nova Scotia in 1785. Frederictonians liked to think that they were Governor Carleton's "chosen" because they formed a more genteel society than the vulgar merchants of Saint John at the mouth of the river. No doubt Saint Johners sought partial vengeance at a later date by sneering at the pretensions of Fredericton, conferring on it the sobriquet "The Celestial City."

In 1785, the streets of the "new" community were surveyed by Royal Engineers and laid out in a grid pattern. The bank of the river on the South Side was designated as Intervale or "Common Land," and oral tradition gave it the name of "The Green." At the turn of the 19th century, Fredericton remained a pretty village. Lady Hunter, the wife of General Martin Hunter, the "president of the province" until 1817, described it as "scattered on a delightful common of the richest sheep pasture I ever saw."

By 1816 the first riverboat, the *General Smyth*, was on the river. Many ferry boats and ferry landings predated the construction of the first bridges, and the river was a hubbub of activity, particularly when the loggers made their way downriver at spring freshet.

This background of history will stimulate your imagination as you begin the trek upriver. Just beyond the Trans Canada Trail Pavilion, to the left across Queen Street, is Christ Church Cathedral. It is no doubt Fredericton's most significant structure, both architecturally and historically. Bishop John Medley was instrumental in having the cathedral built on this site; it was the first British cathedral built on a new foundation since the Norman Conquest. It is marked by a Historic Sites and Monuments Board of Canada monument. Tours of the cathedral are available during the summer months.

Beyond the cathedral, where King Street meets Queen Street, is the cenotaph to Frederictonians who died in World War I, World War II, and the Korean Conflict. Further on, at 776 Queen Street, across from the St. Andrew's Society's Robbie Burns statue, is Farraline Place, the last house before the government buildings. It was built by Peter Fraser, a Scottish fur trader, in 1791. Many features, including the dormers, were added later. It is now a senior citizens' home.

Next to Farraline Place, across from the Green, is the New Brunswick Legislative Assembly precinct. The Legislative Building was built in 1882, replacing the wooden Province Hall which had burned on the same site two years earlier. It is interesting to note that both Saint John and Moncton had offered to build legislatures in their respective cities after the fire. Among the major attractions of the Legislative Building are the Victorian legislative chamber and, in the Legislative Library, an elephant folio of 435 hand-coloured copperplate engravings of birds by John James Audubon. Several of these were sketched in New Brunswick. There are daily tours in English and French during the summer months, and the building is open during normal office hours throughout the year.

The companion two-storey stone structure on the downriver side of the Legislative Building was built in 1816 as an office for the Provincial Secretary; at that time it had only one storey. It is the oldest surviving public building in Fredericton, and it is said to be haunted.

Retracing your footsteps to the Green, you can catch a glimpse of the Playhouse beyond the Legislative Building, on the corner of St. John and Queen streets, before you follow the trail behind the Beaverbrook Art Gallery. Both the Playhouse and the Gallery were given to the province and city by Lord Beaverbrook. The Gallery is internationally known for its collection of British paintings from Elizabethan times to the present, and Salvador Dali's *Santiago el Grande* and the extensive Cornelius Kreighoff collection attract visitors from around the world. Atlantic Canadian painters are featured in the upriver wing, the Marion McCain Gallery, added in 1994. There is a small admission charge.

There is so much to see from the Green, and access can be gained to so many places from it. Beyond the McCain addition to the Gallery, at the riverbank, are the Lord Beaverbrook Hotel and the Regent Street Marina. The imitation lighthouse is a recent and rather controversial addition to the landscape.

On November 4, 1996, Fredericton City Council designated a section of the trail running upriver along the Green from Regent Street as Limpert Lane. The name honours Marianne Limpert, a Frederictonian who won the 1996 Olympic silver medal in the 200-metre individual medley swimming event. Limpert Lane continues along the Green for about a kilometre to a point just below the New Brunswick Peace Officers' Memorial. Other monuments and recent constructions will catch your eye as you proceed. Historical photographs mounted on pedestals provide interesting insights into things as they once were. Kilometre signposts are also posted along the trail.

As you proceed from the foot of Regent Street, you will see in the river the piers of the old Carleton Street Bridge, which was replaced upriver by the Westmorland Street Bridge in the early 1980s. A committee has proposed to install a "Silver Fountain" on one of the piers to honour New Brunswick athletes, and work is continuing to achieve this. Artistic displays were mounted on three of the piers in the summer of 1998 under the auspices of the Beaverbrook Art Gallery, commemorating Fredericton's 150th Anniversary.

To the left, the Military Compound stretches out parallel with the river, encompassing the city blocks north of Queen Street from Regent Street to York Street. British troops manned the garrison in this compound from 1785 to 1869. They were replaced, after the compound was used briefly for other purposes, by a Canadian garrison. The most prominent building of the Military Compound to be seen from the Green is the Officers' Quarters (c. 1839) on Officers' Square. It now houses the York-Sunbury Historical Society Museum, open during scheduled hours from April to December and by appointment from January to March. You must at some point during your stay in Fredericton see the 19-kilogram (42-pound) stuffed Coleman Frog in this museum. (See also Killarney Lake, pages 91-94.)

Other buildings in the Military Compound include the New Brunswick Sports Hall of Fame, the Soldiers' Barracks, the Guardhouse, the Militia Arms Store and former military hospital, and the contemporary Fredericton Public Library. All are well worth visiting. Not much of the detail of the compound can be seen from the trail, but it is there, and it has much to offer. The pedway across St. Anne Point Drive at Carleton Street makes the compound more readily accessible by safely connecting it with this part of the trail.

You will pass to the rear of City Hall on the corner of York and Queen streets — it's the Victorian building with the clock tower. Constructed in 1875, it is the oldest City Hall in Atlantic Canada still maintaining its original use. At one time the upper floor was a theatre and opera house, and today's Council Chamber occupies this space, tastefully and lovingly restored. Inside the chamber, on permanent display, are a series of tapestries designed by Gertrude Duffie and hand-woven by Dr. Ivan H. Crowell; these depict major events in the history of Fredericton.

Upriver from the Westmorland Street Bridge is the Small Craft Aquatic Centre. This centre has done a great deal to augment activities on the St. John River, and it offers canoe and kayak rentals. The Fredericton Rowing Club, which operates from these premises, has already acquired a national reputation and is on the verge of establishing international standing.

A short rise in the elevation of the trail leads into a beautiful grove of pine trees. These trees mark the Old Government House property. Old Government House itself was built in 1828 and has recently been restored. It resumed its proper place in New Brunswick history in 1999 when, for the first time since the 1890s, when Lieutenant-Governor Sir Samuel Leonard Tilley removed his effects and moved home to Saint John, it became the lieutenant-governor's permanent residence and office. During the interim years it served as the site of the Deaf and Dumb Institute (the name of which was more acceptable in 1900 than now), as a First World

The Grove and the Sheraton Fredericton Hotel. HAROLD BOONE

War rehabilitation hospital, and as RCMP "J" Division Headquarters.

Old Government House contains a multimedia interpretation centre honouring New Brunswick's founders: the First Nations, the French, and the British peoples. This is most appropriate, as the site is the oldest settled part of Fredericton and is just metres downriver from the location of an early Maliseet and Acadian burial ground. First Nations celebrations continue to take place at various times during the summer on the land between Old Government House and the Sheraton Hotel.

The modern Sheraton Fredericton Hotel provides a comfortable anchor point for the furthest upriver extremity of the Green. One can gain access to the Valley Trail from the Sheraton via Woodstock Road and either Rookwood Avenue or the Hanwell Road.

Parking
Paid parking is available at meters along Queen Street and behind the Library and Officers' Square and in parking lots behind the Lord Beaverbrook Hotel and City

Hall. Free parking is available at the Small Craft Aquatic Centre and the Sheraton Hotel.

The Valley Trail

Length: 9.4 km
Difficulty: easy to
   moderate
Hiking Time: 2 hr

Wheelchair Use: yes
   (grade at Bucket Club)
Direction: east - west

The Valley Trail begins at Smythe Street and continues upriver along the St. John River to the city limits at McIntosh Brook, following the Canadian National Valley Line roadbed, abandoned in the 1960s. It occasionally provides glimpses of wildlife, including muskrat, deer, and osprey and it is particularly suited to cross-country skiing, being generally sheltered by trees.

From Smythe Street the trail passes near the Fredericton Raceway and Exhibition Grounds. It follows an idyllic path upriver through quiet, well-treed suburban areas and past small brooks and waterways, crossing several streets.

Angelview Park, where the trail rejoins the river, provides an interesting stopover and picnic site. The Fredericton Trails Coalition, the local Kiwanis Club, and the city have erected a covered picnic table at this location in memory of Walter J. Dohaney, a past president of the Kiwanis Club and a devoted friend of the trails.

A little further upriver along the Valley Trail is the very enjoyable Edgecombe Park, donated to the city by a descendant of a well-known Fredericton family who owned a popular department store. Many varieties of trees and shrubs define an area restful to the mind and

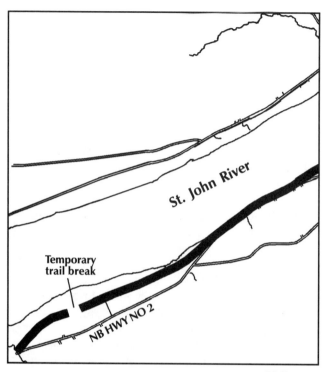

Valley

eye. Still further along the trail is a more commercial endeavour, the Hartt Island Campground and Bucket Club Activity Park, which provides recreational facilities such as canoe rentals, mini-golf, batting cages, water slides, and a driving range, as well as a canteen.

There is a temporary break in the Valley Trail near its end at the Silverwood Sewage Lagoon, in place until a private lease expires. When you get to this spot, please go back to the highway and pick up the trail at the next entry point.

The Fredericton Trails Coalition is attempting to use its mandate to lengthen the Valley Trail. With a number

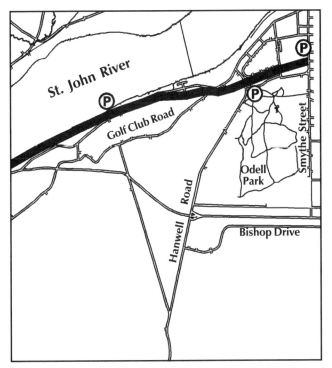

Trail

of other interested parties, it would like to extend the trail downriver (east) of the Smythe Street trailhead across the city from Smythe Street to University Avenue to link up with the Lincoln Trail. The abandoned rail line is blocked in some places, and development proposals for this valuable land are constantly under discussion. The Cross Town Trail Committee has been established to attempt to join the two trails. Also in this area is the derelict York Street Railway Station, which offers a grand opportunity for further trail development, perhaps in collaboration with a private developer. At the upper (western) end, beyond McIntosh Brook, arrangements

The Valley Trail. HAROLD BOONE

are being made with Sentier NB Trail to take the trail to the Mactaquac Fish Hatchery. In the more distant future, it is hoped to progress from there through the Kingsclear First Nation Reserve to the Mactaquac Dam and across the St. John River, connecting with the trails there.

Parking

There are many access points to the trail, and several offer parking. Near the Smythe Street trailhead, you can park at the Exhibition Grounds or at Odell Park. There are several parking spots at the Angelview Park picnic site. If you're coming off the Trans-Canada Highway, you can park behind the Tim Horton's restaurant and the Esso and Irving service stations. Along the Trans-Canada, there's limited parking at the St. John River Anglers' Association roadway, at the Bucket Club, at the roadway to the Silverwood Lagoon just beyond the Roadside Motel, and at McIntosh Brook, where the trail ends.

The Gibson Trail. HAROLD BOONE

The Riverfront Pathway. BILL THORPE

The Marysville/Nashwaak Trail. BILL THORPE

The Gibson Trail

Length: 4.1 km   **Wheelchair Use:** yes
Difficulty: easy   **Direction:** south - north
Hiking Time: 50 min

The Gibson Trail follows the route of the old spur rail line connecting Barker's Point and Marysville, and at its northern end it parallels the Nashwaak River quite closely. The spur line was built by Alexander "Boss" Gibson, the founder of Marysville, to service the Marysville Cotton Mill, and the trail is, of course, named after him. The Gibson Trail begins at Greenwood Drive and ends at the Marysville Heritage Centre and Marysville Place.

You can join the Gibson Trail from the Barker's Point Lions Club on Carman Avenue, proceeding behind the club building along a cleared area until you reach the trail. Or you can begin at the confluence of the north end of the Railway Bridge, the North Side Trail, and the Marysville/Nashwaak Trail at the end of Barker Street. This access adds about a kilometre to the trail's length, but to lighten the burden, luscious blackberries can often be found growing beside the railbeds in late August. You travel east past the sports fields near the site of the South Devon Station and cross the lovely Nashwaak River via the pedestrian bridge, formerly a railway bridge. A portion of this bridge was burned in the early hours of the morning on Sunday, May 17, 1998. This was the first major act of vandalism on the Fredericton trail system. Trail patrols, increased community pressure, bridge lighting, and additional police presence will hopefully address potential problems of this nature. The bridge was promptly repaired with the co-operation of the City of Fredericton, the Island View Correctional Centre, and the Fredericton Trails Coalition.

The Gibson Trail in winter, near the Marysville Heritage Centre.
HAROLD BOONE

After crossing the Nashwaak River, continue straight, right across Greenwood Drive. You may wish to take a 400-metre detour at the Greenwood Drive crossing and follow the street southward toward the St. John River. Here, facing the Fort Nashwaak Motel, there are two memorial cairns. One of the cairns commemorates Loyalist Anthony Barker, after whom Barker's Point is named. The other is a memorial to Barker's Point men killed in World Wars I and II. Strangely enough, the Historic Sites and Monuments Board of Canada cairn, erected in 1926 to mark historic Fort Nashwaak, was placed to the left of the roadway leading to the boat-launching beach in Carleton Park. This location is about 800 metres up the St. John River from the mouth of the Nashwaak River, where the fort is thought to have been built.

Near the Barker's Point end of the Gibson Trail, at Victory Avenue, you'll come to the lower end of a mean-dering 1-kilometre trail through the Hyla Park Nature Preserve, once a sand and gravel quarry and now

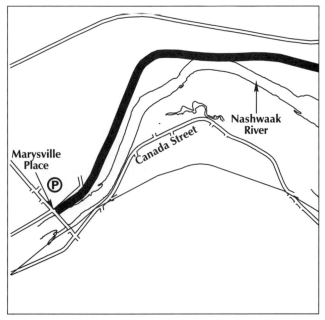

Gibson

Canada's first amphibian park. It has been established "to properly protect the Barker's Point grey tree frog population and habitat." Hyla Park is the most northeasterly known habitat of the grey tree frog in North America. The park entrance is a little further along the Gibson Trail, behind the Greenwood Drive Baptist Church parking lot. On October 3, 1998, a kiosk marking the Hyla Park entrance was formally opened. The diversion is worthwhile, although the park is low-lying, and its paths are subject to flooding in the spring and during wet periods. For more information, the Nature Trust of New Brunswick has prepared an excellent pamphlet, *Hyla Park Nature Preserve: Canada's First Amphibian Park,* usually available in the kiosk.

As it heads north, much of the Gibson Trail is bor-

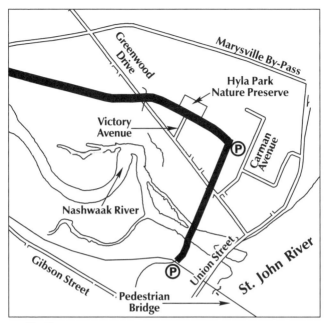

Trail

dered by woods which provide particularly beautiful fall and spring scenery. The sheltered nature of this part of the trail makes it highly suitable for winter walking and cross-country skiing.

As the trail approaches Marysville, it begins to cross idyllic pasture land, interrupted to the left by the lazily flowing Nashwaak River, bordered by tall elms, colourful maples, and sweeping willows. During spring freshet the Nashwaak flows rather more rambunctiously, but it poses no danger other than occasional obvious flooding. The steel bars built into the trail treadway periodically are meant to discourage livestock from using the trail as an escape route from the pastures, and they are easily traversed by human feet, bicycles, skis, and wheel-chairs.

While following the Nashwaak River across the meadows, you begin to notice Marysville ahead. Eventually the four-storey, 127-metre-long former cotton mill comes into view. Now resurrected as Marysville Place, it provides offices for the provincial government. The state-of-the-art mill opened on June 13, 1885. It boasted 18,648 panes of glass in 518 arched windows, which are visible today.

The mill was built with brick from Gibson's own Marysville brickyard, and the same brick was also used to construct the mill-owned tenements for employees, still very much in evidence. At 5:50 every morning the bell in the mill's 40-metre tower rang to waken employees, and it rang again at 6:50, at which time they were expected to be on the job. Inside Marysville Place is a statue of "Boss" Gibson, along with tapestries by Susan Judah depicting the various eras of Marysville history.

At the upriver end of the old mill, you can cross the bridge and join the Marysville/Nashwaak Trail.

Parking

Parking is available at the site of the old South Devon Station, at the Barker's Point Lions Club, in the Greenwood Drive Baptist Church lot, at the Marysville Heritage Centre, and at or near Marysville Place. These are all dedicated or private parking areas and should be respected as such.

Marysville/Nashwaak Trail

Length: 7.4 km   **Wheelchair Use:** yes
Difficulty: easy   **Direction:** south - north
Hiking Time: 1 hr 30 min

The Marysville/Nashwaak Trail, a joint designation reflecting a compromise between the city and Sentier NB Trail, was added to the trail system in the summer of 1997, taking advantage of an abandoned railbed. This railway had begun as the Northern and Western Railway of New Brunswick in 1887 , linking South Devon with Chatham. Under the ownership of Alexander "Boss" Gibson and his partners, it later became the Canada Eastern Railway, and, eventually, part of the Canadian National Railway system. It was last used as a railway in April, 1995.

The trail begins at the north side of the Fredericton Railway Bridge. Travelling in a northerly direction over the North Side underpass, with the Irving Oil tanks on the right, you will notice the stone platform and parking area of the now-razed South Devon Station about 200 metres along on the left. A curved trail leads to the right, passing the city soccer pitches and crossing the Nashwaak River, via the Barker's Point pedestrian bridge, to join the south end of the Gibson Trail.

Keep straight on across Barker Street toward the arch adjoining the Devon Lumber Company property. Devon Lumber has proven to be a great friend of the trail by constructing the entrance arch to the Marysville/ Nashwaak Trail and establishing plantings, fences, and landscaping to mark the trailhead. The official opening of this section took place on October 2, 1998. As you approach the entrance arch, the North Side Trail branches off to the left (see pages 69-74).

The Marysville/Nashwaak Trail follows the edge of

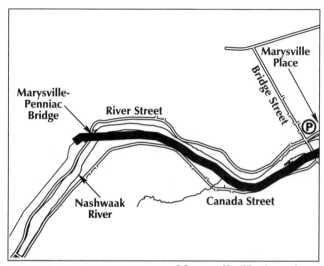

Marysville/Nashwaak

the lumberyard, which offers that very healthy New Brunswick smell of softwood logs, sawdust, and freshly-cut lumber. The area is a former railway marshalling yard, and it adapted readily to its new purpose. On the right the trail is heavily screened by bushes, affording only glimpses of the lush Nashwaak Valley, and it essentially remains so until it crosses Canada Street in Marysville. At this point back yards and broader vistas come into view.

Eventually, you re-cross Canada Street to pass through a park containing the Marysville war memorials. This park marks the site of the railway station last used by the CNR. Unfortunately, nothing remains of that station. At the crossing of Canada Street, the Nashwaak River again comes into view, with Marysville Place, still called the Old Cotton Mill by many, dominating the landscape on the opposite bank. If you like, you can complete a loop with the Gibson Trail by crossing over the bridge at Bridge Street.

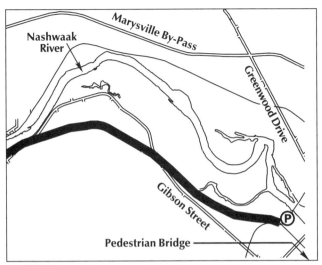

Trail

As you approach Bridge Street you will see some of the more prominent residences of Marysville on your left on the continuation of Canada Street. Old-time residents still refer to this area as Nob Hill in reference to the "upper class" of mill employees and to the upper echelons of the Marysville hierarchy who lived there. The workers' houses, many of which can be seen from the trail, were usually made of brick. Much simpler two-family dwellings, they are mainly on the other side of the Nashwaak River. Nearly all owe their existence to Alexander "Boss" Gibson, who founded Marysville, named it after his wife, and built the mill.

Marysville is well worth a separate visit. It has been designated a National Historic Site by the Historical Sites and Monuments Board of Canada. A small, well-illustrated guidebook, *A Tour of Boss Gibson's Marysville, A Nineteenth Century Mill Town*, is available at local bookstores and at the York-Sunbury Historical Society Museum downtown.

Marysville in the 1880s, with the Cotton Mill in the background.
PANB P5-318A, GEORGE T. TAYLOR COLLECTION

The Marysville/Nashwaak Trail carries on for about 2.5 kilometres beyond Bridge Street to the abandoned railway bridge crossing the Nashwaak River below Penniac. This part of the trail, closely following the Nashwaak past the ruins of a mill dam and through mixed hardwood and evergreen, is felt by some to be one of the more peaceful and beautiful sections of Fredericton's trails. The Marysville-Penniac railway bridge has been converted to pedestrian use, and the jurisdiction of the city of Fredericton ends a few hundred metres beyond it. Soon trail users will be able to travel to Miramichi City via this route as part of the New Brunswick trail system.

Parking
Parking is available at various locations along the route, notably at the South Devon Station site near Devon Lumber and in central Marysville along Mill and Miller streets. River Street, at the northern end of the trail bridge near Penniac, is very narrow, and you must take care to park off the pavement.

Riverfront Pathway

Length: 2.0 km   **Wheelchair Use:** yes
Difficulty: easy   **Direction:** east - west
Hiking Time: 20 min

The Riverfront Pathway runs beside the river on Fredericton's North Side; it parallels Riverside Drive. Essentially, the pathway follows the river along the bank opposite the Green. From it you can obtain an excellent view of the downtown Fredericton skyline across the river. The pathway begins at the Carleton Street Bridge piers, passes under the Westmorland Street Bridge, and then proceeds westward beyond the Loyalists Rugby Clubhouse to Nashwaaksis Place.

The Loyalists Clubhouse and playing fields are indeed aptly named. Caleb Jones, a prominent Loyalist, owned the land from the Nashwaaksis Stream to a spot one mile downriver along the St. John. The present trail winds its way through land formerly in his possession. This same Caleb Jones advertised in the New Brunswick *Royal Gazette*, on October 10, 1786, offering a $6 reward for runaway slaves. The Loyalists Rugby Club purchased this property, which had earlier formed part of the Gill Lumber Mill, and has built a clubhouse and two fields, with the prospect of a third on the upriver side.

The trail ends near the back of Nashwaaksis Place in an area yet to be landscaped. It might seem a logical extension to walk the Riverfront Pathway together with the Johnston Avenue Environmental Park, and there is a connection of sorts because of their proximity. However, for me, there is a definite physical and mental break between the two. The Riverfront Pathway also connects easily with the North Side Trail as it crosses Brookside Drive near Main Street at the Nashwaaksis Commons.

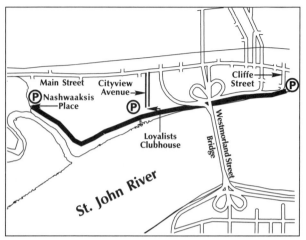

The Riverfront Pathway

Much work is underway to extend the trail and to add to the amenities of the area. In October, 1998, *The Fredericton Daily Gleaner* announced the beginning of plans to develop four soccer pitches and a clubhouse in the area beside the Nashwaaksis Stream. Final plans are yet to be worked out and must include the city's present use of the site, the former Pugh property, to pile snow removed from city streets.

Plans to extend the trail downriver from the piers of the old Carleton Street Bridge to Carleton Park include a ramp from the Railway Bridge to the Park. In the near future Fredericton expects to have a trail system beside the St. John River on the North Side similar in length to the Green on the South Side.

Parking

There is parking space available on the streets near the Carleton Street Bridge piers. Good parking is also available near the Loyalists Clubhouse, access to it being from Cityview Avenue, off Main Street. The city is at present constructing additional parking facilities and a landscaped area adjacent to the clubhouse. Pedestrian access and limited parking are also available from Hillcourt Drive near Beairsto's Family Restaurant, and there is good parking at Nashwaaksis Place.

North Side Trail

Length: 10.5 km   **Wheelchair Use:** yes
Difficulty: moderate   **Direction:** east - west
    (many crossings)
Hiking Time: 2 hr 15 min

The North Side Trail begins near the site of the South Devon Station and to the left of the archway near the end of Barker Street, not far from the north end of the Fredericton Railway Bridge. It follows the old railbed upriver to the city limits at the Carlisle Road. From that point the Douglas Recreation Association takes responsibility for the trail as far as the Keswick Road crossing. In 1998 further construction opened up a greater length of trail to Burtts Corner, Millville, and beyond. The North Side Trail forms part of the Irving Trail, the 377-kilometre stretch of the Trans Canada Trail from Grand Falls to Fredericton, which was donated to the New Brunswick trail system by J.D. Irving Limited.

The North Side Trail begins in the area of Fredericton called Devon, a separate village that amalgamated with Fredericton in 1948. The railway played an integral part in the life of the community until its demise in the 1980s. The sod was turned for the construction of this railbed, belonging to the New Brunswick Land and Railway Company, in 1873. It later became part of the Canadian

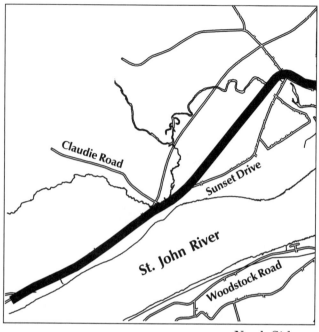

North Side

Pacific Railway system and was known as the Gibson Branch.

The trail first passes the Devon Lumber Company on the right. The neat fencing and the entrance arch to the Marysville/Nashwaak Trail on the right were donated by Devon Lumber. The trail crosses Gibson Street not far from Joe's Diner, where Boyd and Helen MacTavish have been serving great food and banter to Northsiders, and even the occasional Southsider, for well over 30 years.

The trail passes ball fields and tennis courts near the Devon Middle School off to the right. A portion of the abandoned rail line has provided a safe walkway for the students of the school for some time, making it a prime section for the Fredericton Trails Coalition's Adopt A Trail

Trail

Program. Any school or group that joins the Adopt A Trail Program carries out clean-up duties along a designated section of trail, and its name is placed on signs at the beginning and end of its section.

As you continue upriver you will see the St. Mary's Maliseet First Nation Band Office on the right. The Maliseet people have been and remain a very important part of the life of the city of Fredericton. They formerly occupied a very small piece of land — only 2 1/4 acres — on the bank of the St. John River, but they moved to the present 340-acre site in 1928. It is the "new" site that can be seen from the trail, which, in fact, crosses First Nations land here.

One of the pioneer First Nations people recorded to

have settled permanently in the St. Mary's area was Gabriel Acquin, who probably came from the Aukpaque area, a part of Fredericton a short distance upriver on the South Side, in 1847. He achieved great fame as a hunter, a guide, and an expert canoeist. When the Prince of Wales was visiting at Government House in 1860, he had the benefit of a canoe ride on the St. John River with Gabe. Gabe was later invited to London, where he displayed his prowess with the canoe.

Proceeding upriver from Devon, the pathway crosses under the approach to the Westmorland Street Bridge. It parallels Main Street in the Nashwaaksis area of the city, passing through well-established neighbourhoods and back yards and to the rear of the business premises, providing a link between the Main Street businesses and the residential areas on the other side of the trail.

Where the trail meets Brookside Drive, at a mini-park containing facilities built by Youth Services Canada, you can cross Main Street to Ferry Avenue and the Nashwaaksis Commons at Nashwaaksis Place. A connection can be made there with both the Riverfront Pathway (see pages 67-68) and the Johnston Avenue Environmental Park trail (see pages 88-89).

At the intersection of the Royal Road and the trail, you can see the picturesque Stone Bridge to the left, where the Royal Road, Sunset Drive, and Main Street meet, clearly an important intersection, both historic and contemporary. The Stone Bridge was built in 1937, replacing a covered bridge which was at that location.

Nashwaaksis (its name, accented on the last syllable, derives from the Maliseet word for "slowly moving current") was a centre busy enough to rival Fredericton, its mills and ancillary businesses making it a hub of activity. Of these businesses few signs can be seen from the trail. The MacFarlane Works, a foundry near Brookside Drive, was probably the best known. It must have

Elementary school children enjoy the North Side Trail near Brookside Drive. NB TRAILS COUNCIL INC.

been near the trail, because local historian Ruth Scott says in her book *Nashwaaksis 1765-1973: A History* that the foundry had to be moved when the railway was built in 1872. Although the main factory eventually moved to Fredericton, a blacksmith shop remained in Nashwaaksis. It grew to become MacFarlane's Wagon Factory, closing in 1933. Nashwaaksis and Fredericton were first connected by ferries and later by bridges. In 1973, the town joined with Marysville and Barker's Point to amalgamate with Fredericton.

Except for occasional glimpses near the Westmorland Street Bridge, you almost lose sight of the St. John River on the North Side Trail, and in fact you lose contact with a watercourse of any consequence until you reach the Nashwaaksis Stream just above the Stone Bridge. At this point you cross the stream, a very swift and exciting one during spring freshet, via a railway bridge which has been converted to trail use.

From here the trail passes through wooded areas bordering on newer subdivisions until it crosses Sunset Drive. Off to the left just after that crossing, in among the trees, is a former summer cottage colony on Claremont Drive, the buildings now converted to year-round homes.

After the Carlisle Road, at the city boundary, the St. John River comes into view again and some wonderful vistas appear, often framed in magnificent pine trees.

Parking

Parking is available at many locations, since in its 10.5 kilometres the North Side Trail meets streets at approximately 30 points. Be very careful when parking as well as when crossing these streets. In 1999, these street crossings were marked by the city with well-made and aesthetically pleasing red and white signs.

Recreational Trails

Odell Park. CITY OF FREDERICTON, TOURISM

Nashwaaksis Field House Trail. RYAN ASTLE

Johnston Street Environmental Park. HAROLD BOONE

Odell Park

Length: 9.2 km (hiking and ski trails)
16 km (hiking and ski trails plus footpaths)
Difficulty: easy to strenuous
Hiking Time: varies

Wheelchair Use: only the Arboretum section
Direction: mainly north - south

Odell Park is named after Jonathan Odell, a Loyalist whose satirical verse made him one of the foremost propagandists during the American Revolution. He studied medicine at Princeton University and pursued a chequered career that included stints as a British army surgeon, a clergyman and the chaplain of the King's American Dragoons, a United Empire Loyalist, and New Brunswick's first Provincial Secretary. Around 1785, he built the house still standing at the corner of Brunswick and Church streets, now owned by the Anglican Diocese of Fredericton and used as the Christ Church Cathedral Deanery. Jonathan Odell was godfather to Clement C. Moore, who wrote the poem "A Visit from St. Nicholas," now known as "The Night Before Christmas." Moore sent Odell an early copy.

In area, Odell Park is slightly more than 300 acres, and it was one of the first land grants awarded near what is now Fredericton. The title to this estate, which was called Rookwood, remained with descendants of the Odell family until January 9, 1942, when the City of Fredericton purchased it for $12,000. At the request of the city, a provincial act was passed in 1954 creating a public park to be known as Odell Park, and the city passed its own bylaw respecting use of the park in 1963.

Odell Park remains today as Fredericton's "crown jewel," enhanced by the addition of lawns, duck ponds,

The Rookwood Estate house of William Hunter Odell, Jonathan Odell's grandson. This house burned in 1946. Odell Park Lodge now occupies the site. PANB P5-273, GEORGE T. TAYLOR COLLECTION

a large deer enclosure, barbecue pits, picnic tables, children's play equipment, and a multi-purpose visitors' centre, Odell Park Lodge, opened by the Queen Mother in 1967. The Fredericton Pony Club maintains its headquarters and stables to the left of the park entrance, just beyond the caretaker's house. Horses are permitted on certain marked trails.

As well as the main entrance at the bottom of the park off Rookwood Avenue, there are also entrances near the top. Off Smythe Street, opposite Willingdon Street, follow the sign for Thompson Field Baseball Park. Two very pleasant accesses to Odell Park are through the Fredericton Botanic Garden. You may enter off Prospect Street, between Smythe Street and Hanwell Road, at the bottom of the Prospect Street Ball Field parking lot, or from Cameron Court, off Hanwell Road, at the Botanic Garden headquarters.

Odell Park has 16 kilometres of trail for use by pedestrians, cyclists, horseback riders and skiers. It is heavily forested, in many places with original-growth trees. It is

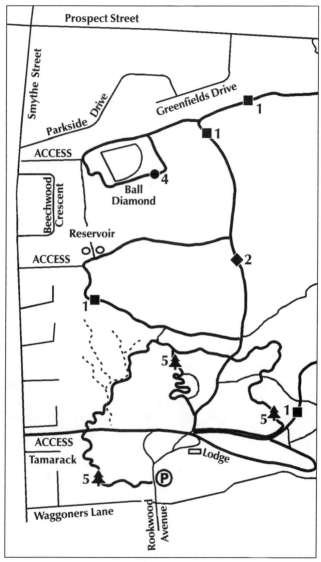

Odell

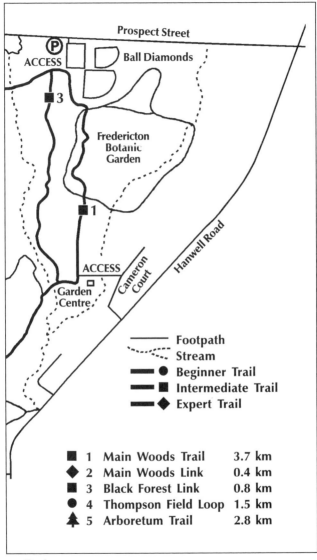

Prospect Street

ACCESS

Ball Diamonds

3

Fredericton
Botanic
Garden

1

ACCESS

Hanwell Road

Cameron Court

Garden
Centre

——— Footpath
.... Stream
■■■● Beginner Trail
■■■■ Intermediate Trail
■■■◆ Expert Trail

■ 1 Main Woods Trail   3.7 km
◆ 2 Main Woods Link   0.4 km
■ 3 Black Forest Link   0.8 km
● 4 Thompson Field Loop 1.5 km
▲ 5 Arboretum Trail   2.8 km

Park

Odell Park. CITY OF FREDERICTON, TOURISM

also very steep in the upper hillside area, and consequently the trails demand a rather high skill level among skiers. Bicycles are banned from the steep slopes because they create ruts, which lead to trail degradation and washouts. At the lower level of the park, the Odell Arboretum displays various types of New Brunswick trees and shrubs.

The trails used for skiing are named, and the signs that mark them indicate their degree of difficulty for skiers. Walkers may use these signs to estimate difficulty due to steepness; in addition, the trails on the upper slopes may present such stumbling blocks as rocks, exposed roots, and wet spots. The Odell Arboretum paths are level, wide, and well groomed, ideal for wheelchairs.

Parking

There is a big parking lot at the lower entrance off Rookwood Avenue and another at the Prospect Street Ball Field, and there is more limited parking at the other entrances.

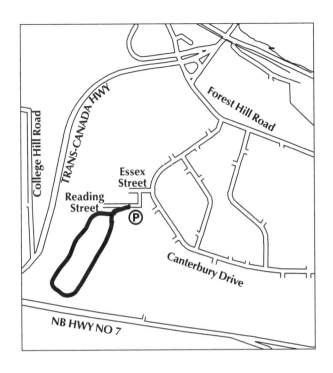

Reading Street Park Trail

Length: 1.1 km only
Difficulty: easy
Hiking Time: 15 min

Wheelchair Use: in parts only
Direction: loop

Reading Street Park is a gem of a trail. While you're walking it, you'll have a hard time imagining that you're in the city. In fact, the park, while bounded by busy, fast highways and bustling subdivisions, is really an extension of the University of New Brunswick Woodlot, the lovely sylvan belt that wraps around the south of Fredericton.

The trail begins near the Reading Street Park sign. The surface is not crusher-dusted, but it is in excellent shape, with no protruding roots to trip you. The slight uphill grade throughout much of its length and the distinct slope near the end may pose a problem for wheelchairs. There are a few rather narrow and uneven side trails. All in all, it's simply a very pleasant, easy walk, not far from the centre of town.

The Reading Street Park Trail can be accessed from Forest Hill Road: drive east and uphill from the Princess Margaret Bridge, turn right onto Canterbury Drive, right onto Essex Street, then left onto Reading Street. The entrance is well marked. There are no garbage containers and no amenities on the trail.

Parking

There is ample parking near flower plantings and a large field.

UNB Woodlot and Game Refuge

Length: hiker's preference
Difficulty: easy to
  moderate
Hiking Time: hiker's
  preference

Wheelchair Use: generally no
Direction: not specific

The University of New Brunswick Woodlot has provided recreation for generations of Frederictonians during all seasons of the year. It is a block of freehold forest land approximately 3563 acres in size, "situated south of the [old] Trans-Canada Highway, bounded on the north and east by the City of Fredericton, on the south by the Parish of New Maryland, and on the west by the Parish of Kingsclear and the City of Fredericton" (Geoplan, 1990). The Woodlot is part of the original grant given to the College of New Brunswick by King George III in 1800.

The woodlot is first and foremost a teaching, research, and demonstration facility used by the UNB Faculty of Forestry and the Departments of Biology and Geodesy and Geomatic Engineering and by the Maritime Forest Ranger School. Many individual scientific and practical projects are underway at various times of the year. It is a busy place, well populated by both professional and recreational users. In addition to the ongoing projects, over 80,000 cords of wood have been harvested between 1914 and 1983, much of the harvesting experimental and done with a teaching bias. Recreational uses include walking, running, birdwatching, cycling, horseback riding, cross-country skiing, snowshoeing, and snowmobiling.

It must be emphasized that the recreational use of the woodlot has been with the forbearance of the university and its management delegate, the Maritime Forest Ranger School. Neither institution has actively promoted or discouraged such use, and neither assumes responsibility for inconvenience, injury, or damage sustained by individuals or their vehicles or other property here. The priority uses of the woodlot were determined by the UNB Board of Governors in 1950; no money has been set aside for development of recreational facilities, and no map is available at this time.

The woodlot road and trail systems are extensive. This system serves all users, so you may encounter anyone from a silent birdwatcher to tree harvesters to a class of students as you explore the paths. The woodlot is not under the supervision of the City of Fredericton, and therefore the by-laws established for the use of linear parks in the city do not apply. Use the area with care, both for yourself and for your surroundings. I have walked, skied, and cycled over most of the trails, and I have always felt privileged to be there.

At the north end of the woodlot, opposite the Regent Mall, is what is locally known as the Forestry Complex; officially, it's the Hugh John Flemming Forestry Centre, which was opened in 1988. It includes the Maritime Forest Ranger School, the New Brunswick Department of Natural Resources and Energy, the federal Department of Forestry, and the University of New Brunswick Tweeddale Centre for Forest Industrial Research, as well as other forestry associations. The main entrance to the woodlot is here.

The Fredericton Trails Coalition began talking with the Village of New Maryland as early as 1997 to attempt to connect the New Maryland trail system with the city along Route 101, which bisects the woodlot, and to ensure a route past the new Trans-Canada Highway at the woodlot's south boundary. Both the village and the city will, of course, have to work out the details of such a system with the University of New Brunswick.

Parking

The only parking is along the entrance road to the Hugh John Fleming Forestry Centre off Regent Street; simply drive to the end of the road and leave your car on the roadside. This is not a parking lot, and it is private property, so be considerate as well as careful.

Kingswood

Length: 2.5 km (20 km planned)

Difficulty: easy to moderate

Hiking Time: 20 min (1999)

Wheelchair Use: no

Direction: tandem west - east loops (planned)

Kingswood is a private development, open to the general public on a user-pay basis. It is located on an 800-acre site off the Hanwell Road on the southern boundary of Fredericton, and it is still in the process of being developed. A large sign is easy to see on the left side of the Hanwell Road about 2.5 kilometres beyond the intersection of Prospect Street and the Hanwell Road.

Kingswood will have 20 kilometres of trail when completed, and it will be divided into nine more-or-less tandem loops. Three of these loops, each 2.5 km long, near the main building, will be developed to provide cross-country skiing during the winter of 1999-2000. The loops will offer double tracked, one-way groomed trails which will be double the width of the Fredericton system, that is, 6.1 metres (20 feet). Skating ponds are a future possibility.

The loops will be crusher-dusted for use during other times of the year by walkers, runners, and cyclists. There is to be a 27-hole golf course and a driving range. The first loop of the trail system, which is already built, passes under the newly constructed portion of the Trans-Canada Highway.

The Kingswood indoor facility covers nearly two acres and offers bowling, gymnastics, a fitness centre, a canteen, a banquet room, a child-care area, and a sports medicine centre. Some call Kingswood the most highly developed fitness centre in Atlantic Canada. In 1998,

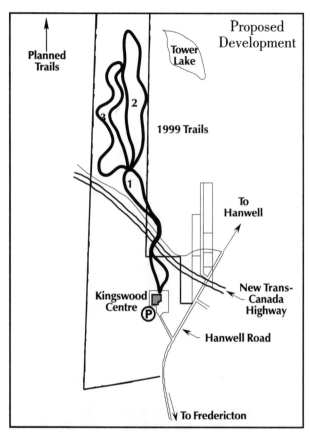

Kingswood

Gymnastics Canada Gymnastique selected Kingswood to be the home of the Canadian men's gymnastics team.

Parking
Kingswood has a large parking lot.

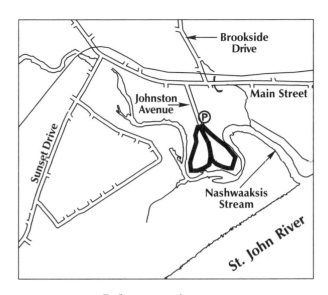

Johnston Avenue
Environmental Park Trail

Length: 1.1 km
Difficulty: easy
Hiking Time: 15 min

Wheelchair Use: no
Direction: loop

The Johnston Avenue Environmental Park Trail is behind Nashwaaksis Place in the park at the end of Johnston Avenue between Main Street and the St. John River. Proceed beyond the Nashwaaksis Arena and two ball fields toward a sign proclaiming, "Main Street Environmental Park."

Summer and fall are the best times to enjoy this trail. The area is a low flood plain surrounded on three sides by the Nashwaaksis Stream, which floods during almost every spring freshet. Even when spring is early and dry, the main trail can be muddy enough to provide a bit of adventure, and the side trails will be too muddy to travel.

It requires little imagination to expect alligators to rise out of the primeval ooze. Bicycling is not recommended at this time of year. But the wetness means that bird life is abundant, and a beaver once slapped its tail as I approached.

The main trail is not well marked by signs, but is easy to follow, and the area is so small and self-contained that there is no possibility of losing your way. Indeed, mosquitoes are probably the most relevant danger, due largely to the amount of still water. I saw a middle-aged man and woman scurrying from the trail one day as I was leaving; they had worn shorts and were paying for their mistake as the hordes attacked. As its name implies, this area is treasured for its environmental value. Inconvenient as mosquitoes and mud may be to humans, the area is a rich habitat for plant and animal life and should be left in its natural state.

It is most comfortable to walk the trail later in the year, when it may not be necessary to bring along your insect repellent. In summer the lush greenery is thoroughly rewarding. The trails are dry, and the low trees and tall grasses are reminiscent of a more accessible Okefenokee Swamp. Frederictonians often walk through its coolness in the evenings. In October the mosquitoes are all gone, the fall colours are in their full glory, the trail is dry and leaf-carpeted, and large flocks of southbound geese will take off at your approach.

Parking
Public free parking is plentiful within metres of the trailhead.

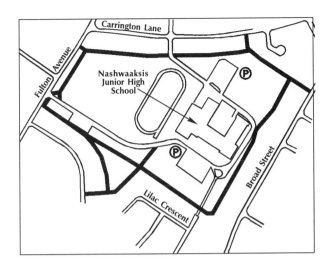

Nashwaaksis Field House Trail

Length: 1.5 km
Difficulty: easy
Hiking Time: 15 min

Wheelchair Use: no
Direction: loop

This trail loops around the Nashwaaksis Middle School and Field House. It proceeds through open and partly wooded areas with several access and exit points. I would characterize this as a neighbourhood trail, its proximity to schools, sports facilities, and residential areas making it a convenient and pleasant pedestrian thoroughfare. Its many access points lead to other shorter, but official, trails through the neighbouring yards and across one very large grassed park with a children's playground.

Although this trail has the same 3.05-metre (10-foot) width as the rest of the Fredericton trails system, it is not crusher-dusted, the treadway being of a larger gravel composition. The grades are not steep, but some would

The Nashwaaksis Field House Trail is a popular neighbourhood path. BILL THORPE

no doubt be difficult for wheelchair use, and the coarse surface would also pose difficulties.

The facilities of the Nashwaaksis Field House, the community library, and the Fredericton Indoor Pool are used extensively by Frederictonians and offer attractions for the visiting trail user as well.

Parking

There is plenty of free parking near the recently constructed soccer and rugby fields and in front of and behind the school. Please do not occupy space near the school when school is in session.

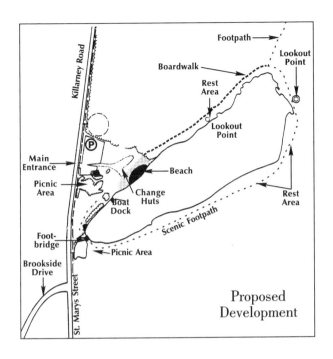

Killarney Lake

Length: 1.5 km (planned)   **Wheelchair Use:** part
Difficulty: easy to   **Direction:** loop
    moderate
Hiking Time: 20 min

Killarney Lake Park is still actually a park in the making, even though Killarney Lake has provided Frederictonians with a recreational facility for decades. *The Killarney Lake Park and Recreation Area Conceptual Plan*, prepared in 1985 by city planners, recommends an excellent and ambitious phased development of the park as funds become available. The city has already begun the process and has expended $20,000 per year for several years on

Killarney Lake, with the sandy beach in the background. BILL THORPE

that development. The first phase of the trail portion of the park is planned for 1999; my description corresponds with that plan.

Killarney Lake is on the city's North Side about five kilometres from the St. John River. It can be reached by driving north on St. Marys Street and its extension, Killarney Road. Heading north off the Westmorland Street Bridge, turn right at Maple Street, the first set of lights at the end of the bridge, and then left onto St. Marys Street at the next set of lights; this will take you to Killarney Road and the park. An alternative route is to carry on straight along the Ring Road and turn right at Brookside Drive, which leads directly to Killarney Road and the park.

The *Conceptual Plan* says, "Killarney Lake Park is set in a region of mixed Acadian forest. Birch, maple, and poplar, typically found in this forest, are the dominant species within the proposed park area. Spruce and fir, along with hemlock and pine, also occur, although in smaller amounts." Most of the park area has been logged over in the past and is immature forest with some fairly young stands. The plan also mentions the presence of glacial till and of long, narrow ridges called eskers, geological formations uncommon in this area, which would have been deposited here during the Ice Age by streams carrying sand and gravel under the ice sheet. Killarney Lake, fed by small brooks and by springs within the lake itself, used to be the source of water for the town of Devon.

Historically, Killarney Lake had a reputation as a resort, and at one time there was a hotel on the site. It has been "the old swimming hole" for decades, if not a century. Present development is limited to approximately 400 acres. The sandy lakeshore beach is the only supervised one in the city, with lifeguards on duty during daylight hours, and changing rooms and toilet facilities on-site.

The paths around Killarney Lake, such as they are, have not been groomed for winter usage by the city. This will be done, however, once the trail around the lake has been completed. A skating surface near the beach is cleared each year.

Killarney Lake's greatest claim to fame is that it was the home of the Coleman Frog. This famous frog, weighing 19 kg (42 lb) at its demise, may be seen in a taxidermal state at the York-Sunbury Historical Society Museum on Queen Street. Some critics have called the frog an "imaginative concoction," but Bruce Hutchinson, a well-known Canadian author, after visiting Fredericton during World War II, wrote in *Canada: The Unknown Country*, "the stuffed corpse of a frog . . . is as large as an English bulldog, and is forever grinning shrewdly at the world. He was found in 1885, lived comfortably as a family pet for some years, coming home for meals twice a day, until somebody killed him by dynamiting his lake for bass. . . . There he sits grinning forever in splendid immortality, Frederictonian to the last grain of stuffing."

The animal with the greatest effect on the lake scene today, however, is the beaver. Around Killarney Lake there are many beaver dams and a good deal of swamp. One beaver dam in the 1980s created a body of water one-third the size of Killarney Lake itself. Other kinds of wildlife in the area include deer, moose, racoon, porcupine, and as many as 150 varieties of birds. There are trout in the lake as well.

I started to walk the loop around Killarney Lake on a warm summer day in June, 1998, after a heavy morning rain. The loop was blocked on the west side of the lake, near Killarney Road, by high water. I went to the east side beyond the beach and proceeded along a primitive flagged trail. It was wet and boggy, and I was plagued by mosquitoes. In spite of this, I found my limited expedition an excellent foretaste of what could be. I saw some very large trees and some chest-high ferns. This portion of the trail will be magnificent, particularly if it is left in its natural state.

Perhaps the trail on the other side of the lake could be set up for wheelchair users and cyclists, as well as pedestrians, leaving the eastern side as a purely natural if somewhat rough trail. The entire loop could include a scenic footpath, a pedestrian walkway, a bikeway, and a cross-country ski trail. There are no steep grades around the lake.

Parking
Killarney Lake Park has only one entrance, where there is a good-sized parking lot.

Some Useful Addresses

Nancy Lockerbie, Manager
City of Fredericton Tourism
Fredericton City Hall
397 Queen St., PO Box 130
Fredericton NB E3B 4Y7
Phone: (506) 460-2041
Fax: (506) 460-2042
nancy.lockerbie@city.fredericton.nb.ca

Harold R. Boone
Foreman, Parks and Trees Division
Fredericton City Hall
397 Queen St., PO Box 130
Fredericton NB E3B 4Y7
Phone: (506) 460-2230
Fax: (506) 460-2293

Fredericton Trails Coalition
PO Box 3715, Station B
Fredericton NB E3A 5L7
Phone: (506) 459-1931
nbtrails@nbnet.nb.ca

Kingswood
31 Kingswood Park
Fredericton NB E3C 2L4
Phone: (506) 444-9500
Fax: (506) 444-9505
mcfadzen@nb.sympatico.ca

Scott MacDonald, Executive Director
New Brunswick Trails Council Inc
235 Main St.
Fredericton NB   E3A 1El
Phone: (506) 459-1931 or 1-800-526-7070
Fax: (506) 458-5639
nbtrails@nbnet.nb.ca

Trans Canada Trail Foundation
43 Westminster Ave. N.
Montreal West QC   H4X 1Y8
Phone: 1-800-465-3636
Fax: (514) 485-4541
www.tctrail.ca; info@tctrail.ca

Tree House
124 St. John St.
Fredericton NB E3B 4A7
Phone: (506) 452-1339

York-Sunbury Historical Society Museum
Officers' Square, PO Box 1312
Fredericton NB   E3B 5C8
Phone: (506) 455-6041

To report problems associated with maintenance of the city's trails, call (506) 460-2038. For ski conditions, call (506) 460-2230.

If you would like to join the Fredericton Trails Coalition or the New Brunswick Trails Council, you may purchase a joint membership for $20. Donations to either organization and to the Trans Canada Trails Foundation are tax deductible.

Bibliography

Books

Eiselt, Marianne and H. A. *A Hiking Guide to New Brunswick* (2nd Edition). Fredericton: Goose Lane, 1996.

Fredericton High School Teachers and Students. *Fredericton: A Capital City* (New Brunswick Canada Studies Project). Fredericton, 1975. (Hannah Ingraham's diary)

Fredericton Trails Coalition. [6 articles]. *Today* (supplement to the Fredericton *Daily Gleaner*). May 31 - July 5, 1997.

Geoplan Consultants. *Report on the UNB Woodlot*. Fredericton, 1990.

Halfpenny, H.E. *Atlas of York County, New Brunswick*. Fredericton: Halfpenny, 1878. Reprinted Belleville: Mika Publishing, 1973.

Hutchinson, Bruce. "The Hometown," *Canada: The Unknown Country*. Toronto: Longmans, 1943.

The Killarney Lake Park and Recreation Area Conceptual Plan. Fredericton: City of Fredericton, 1985.

Nason, David. *Railways of New Brunswick*. Fredericton: New Ireland, 1992.

Pond, Douglas Daamon. *The History of Marysville, New Brunswick*. Fredericton, 1983.

Scott, Ruth. *Nashwaaksis (1765-1973): A History*. Fredericton: Capital Free Press, 1986.

Squires, W. Austin. *History of Fredericton: The Last 200 Years*. Fredericton: Centennial, 1980.

Thompson, Colleen Whitney. *Roads to Remember: The Insider's Guide to New Brunswick*. Fredericton: Goose Lane, 1994.

Pamphlets

Some or all of these pamphlets are available at local bookstores, the York-Sunbury Historical Society Museum, the Tree House, tourist bureaus, hotels, and the kiosk at the entrance to the Hyla Park Nature Preserve.

Dallison, Robert. "A Tour of Boss Gibson's Marysville." Fredericton Heritage Trust, 1991.

Fredericton Visitor Guide. Fredericton Tourism, updated yearly.

Fredericton Trails Coalition. "Trail Guide: City of Fredericton." Fredericton: Carrcraft, 1998.

Martin, Gwen. "Hyla Park Nature Preserve." Fredericton: Nature Trust of New Brunswick, n.d.

"Trans Canada Trail." New Brunswick Trails Council Inc.

"Walking Tours of Fredericton, the Colonial Capital." Fredericton Heritage Trust, 1977.

Acknowledgements

I am grateful to Harold Boone, Foreman, Parks and Trees Division, City of Fredericton, for his knowledge of the linear park system and the other Fredericton parks; Robert Lunn, Map Division, Engineering Department, City of Fredericton, for providing the map-work for the yearly brochure produced by Fredericton Trails Coalition and the maps in this book; and to the other members of the City of Fredericton staff, for their unfailingly kind help. Fred Farrell, at the Provincial Archives of New Brunswick, provided intelligent guidance in my search for historic photographs and kindly assisted me in procuring reproductions.

Walter Long, Jr., a retired railwayman from the Canadian National Railway, brought his practical and personal experiences to bear on various aspects of Rails to Trails, and I am particularly grateful for his generosity in sharing his expertise about the railways and the lines that ran through the city. Brian Barchard's photographs of the railway lines in active use lend an exciting dimension to walking where trains used to run, and I appreciate his assistance.

The Canadian Transportation Agency (Hull QC) and the Canadian Pacific Archives (Montreal QC) were helpful in confirming some of the dates in relation to the railway lines. The Annual Reports of the Fredericton Tree Commission were useful in confirming dates for the opening of various trails which had formerly been rail lines.

Goose Lane Editions has performed an admirable job in preparing this book for publication. I would particularly like to extend my thanks to Ray Cronin, who proposed the idea, and to my editors, Laurel Boone and Darrell Mesheau, who kept me "on trail" and more or less on time.

Index

Trail Notes

Trail Notes

Trail Notes